Cyber Storm V:
After Action Report

July 2016

Homeland
Security

Cyber Storm V After Action Report
Table of Contents

EXECUTIVE SUMMARY

Exercise Background

Cyber Storm (CS), the Department's capstone national-level cyber exercise series, provides the framework for the most extensive government-sponsored cybersecurity exercises of its kind. Mandated by Congress, these exercises are part of the Department's ongoing efforts to assess and strengthen cyber preparedness and examine incident response processes. DHS uses the findings from these exercises to advance collective cyber incident response capabilities. They also strengthen information sharing partnerships among federal, state, international, and private sector partners. The National Cybersecurity and Communications Integration Center's (NCCIC) National Cyber Exercise and Planning Program (NCEPP), under the Office of Cybersecurity & Communications (CS&C), sponsors the exercise series.

The CS V goal and objectives included:

Exercise Goal:

- Strengthen cybersecurity preparedness and response capabilities by exercising policies, processes, and procedures for identifying and responding to a multi-sector cyber attack targeting critical infrastructure

Exercise Objectives:

- Continue to exercise coordination mechanisms, information sharing efforts, development of shared situational awareness, and decision-making procedures of the cyber incident response community during a cyber event
- Evaluate relevant policy, statutory, and fiscal issues that govern cyber incident response authorities and resource prioritization
- Provide a forum for exercise participants to exercise, evaluate, and improve the processes, procedures, interactions, and information sharing mechanisms within their organization or community of interest
- Assess the role, functions, and capabilities of DHS and other government entities in a cyber event

The Exercise Planning Team divided the 18-month planning process into five phases to support the planning, execution, and evaluation of the CS V exercise. These included Scoping, Design and Development, Preparation, Conduct, and Evaluation Phases. Within each stage, a series of events, milestones, and general planning goals moved the process forward. Five major planning meetings served as key milestones and provided an opportunity for collaboration across the entire planning community. Throughout the process, planners engaged in cross-community interaction, public–private collaboration, and information sharing to support increased awareness and achieve goals for each phase.

CS V exercise execution included more than 1,200 participants, representing entities from the public and private sectors within the United States and abroad. Participants represented nine Cabinet-level departments, eight full-player states[1], 12 International partners, and nearly 70 private sector companies and coordination bodies. Participation focused on the Information Technology (IT), Communications, Healthcare and Public Health (HPH), and Commercial Facilities (Retail Subsector) critical infrastructure sectors, while also incorporating various levels of play from other critical infrastructure sectors.

Key Achievements

CS V served as a catalyst for learning for the cyber incident response community. Through the exercise planning and execution process, participants:

- Exercised response to a significant cyber incident with support from federal, state, private sector, and international organizations;
- Integrated new stakeholders into a CS national-level capstone exercise, including two new sectors and eight new states – expanding their exposure to cyber response exercises, and providing a foundation for future exercise and improvement efforts;

---

[1] Other state, local, territorial and tribal entities participated through MS-ISAC alerts

- Provided an avenue for sector coordination bodies, such as Information Sharing and Analysis Centers (ISAC) and Information Sharing and Analysis Organizations (ISAO), to test and refine their coordination mechanisms and demonstrate the value of participation or membership;
- Allowed for private sector organizations to use scenario conditions to collaborate on and develop a range potential solutions and discuss these with their government counterparts;
- Raised awareness of attack vectors that may require non-traditional remediation activities (i.e., not blocking), creating a venue for participating organizations to evaluate response options against potential consequences and emphasizing the need for policies and procedures to remain flexible;
- Provided a venue to examine and identify improvements to internal organizational processes and procedures, including how these may feed into sector or national-level response; and
- Of respondents to the After Action Questionnaire (AAQ) 96% indicated that participation in CS V will help them become better prepared to deal successfully with a cyber incident and 85% have cyber incident response plans.

Scenario and Adversary

Players responded to a cyber-specific scenario that leveraged weaknesses in common protocols and services used on the Internet. The scenario included impacts to routing methodology, the Domain Name System (DNS) used to map hostnames to Internet Protocol (IP) addresses, and Public Key Infrastructure (PKI) used to provide authentication and confidentiality. Scenario conditions affected a wide variety of corporate and government systems, medical devices, and payment systems. During scenario play, the malware included a feature that bricked infected systems when players blocked against the malicious IPs. Resolution required a coordinated government and private sector response.

The CS V adversaries incorporated real world threat elements and had the resources, capabilities, and intent to carry out sophisticated and pervasive attacks. Multiple adversaries used the impacts to routing, host name mapping, and authentication to design and deliver attacks against exercise participants. This allowed a diverse set of adversary groups to target CS V players.

Key Findings

Participant feedback and Exercise Planning Team observations recorded throughout the exercise planning, execution, and after action process revealed four high-level findings that affect the cybersecurity community at large. High-level findings and associated discussion incorporate perspectives of CS V participants representing the Federal Government, State and Local Government, coordination bodies, the private sector, and the International community. In particular, the Exercise Planning Team used the exercise Hotwash, Exercise Spot Reports and After Action Questionnaires (AAQ), CS Community after action teleconferences, and the After Action Meeting (AAM) to build out the findings and supporting evidence. Sub-findings and observations support each high-level finding and provide additional detail.

- *Finding 1: A current, national-level plan or framework that has widespread buy-in, adoption, and integration would have formalized and optimized cyber incident response during CS V.*

- *Finding 2: Challenges around information sharing – thresholds, paths, speed of sharing, and liability issues – still exist and need targeted attention.*

- *Finding 3: CS V players displayed increased awareness of the NCCIC's role in information sharing and shared situational awareness and increasingly looked to DHS, the NCCIC, and US-CERT to coalesce information and provide reporting back out. DHS and the NCCIC should build upon this and continue to improve their processes, procedures, and overall capabilities.*

- *Finding 4: As first time Cyber Storm exercise participants, the Healthcare and Public Health Sector and the Retail Subsector both observed the value of increased coordination within the sector, expanded information sharing across affected sectors, and the value of more formalized coordination and reporting mechanisms through entities such as ISACs or ISAOs.*

Conclusion

CS V provided a realistic environment for our national cyber response apparatus to assess cyber incident response capabilities. DHS and participating organizations worked closely to establish the exercise's goal and objectives and design a realistic scenario that allowed stakeholders to address both organizational and national-level objectives. The resulting scenario allowed the community to coordinate a national-level response to a significant cyber incident. As part of exercise play, players identified significant findings and actions at the national, state, sector, and organizational level that the cyber response community should address. Ultimately, CS V served as a tool that allowed the stakeholder community to examine the evolution of cyber response capabilities and identify current gaps and challenges in responding to a coordinated cyber attack with global impacts. As a result, stakeholders have the opportunity to address these findings and bolster cyber response capabilities at an organizational-level, increasing the preparedness of the nation as a whole.

EXERCISE SUMMARY AND FINDINGS

General Overview

After Action Report Purpose

The Cyber Storm V (CS V) After Action Report (AAR) provides a summary of CS V and identifies findings and sub-findings that inform Department of Homeland Security (DHS) and stakeholder improvement activities.

CS V Introduction

Cyber Storm (CS), the Department's capstone national-level cyber exercise series, provides the framework for the most extensive government-sponsored cybersecurity exercises of its kind. Mandated by Congress, these exercises are part of the Department's ongoing efforts to assess and strengthen cyber preparedness and examine incident response processes. DHS uses the findings from these exercises to advance collective cyber incident response capabilities. They also strengthen information sharing partnerships among federal, state, international, and private sector partners. The National Cybersecurity and Communications Integration Center's (NCCIC) National Cyber Exercise and Planning Program (NCEPP), under the Office of Cybersecurity & Communications (CS&C), sponsors the exercise series.

NCEPP successfully executed CS V from its exercise control cell (ExCon) at the United States Secret Service (USSS) Headquarters as well as from distributed player locations from March 7-11, 2016. On March 7, exercise participants conducted communications checks and final preparations. Live exercise play spanned from 0900 EST on March 8 to 1700 EST on March 10. On March 11, planners, players, and stakeholders participated in an Exercise Hotwash.

Exercise Objectives

Planners and stakeholders developed the CS V goal and objectives based on previous exercise experience and findings from Cyber Storms I-IV and National Level Exercise 12. The goal and objectives are inclusive of community concerns and previous issues, and incorporate current community initiatives. The goal and objectives informed the 18-month planning and execution process. DHS and the CS V Exercise Planning Team[2] worked closely with participating organizations throughout the process in order to achieve the goal and objectives. In addition to overarching CS V Exercise objectives, CS Communities developed Community-Specific objectives and used those to scope their play and their scenario development activities. The CS V goal and objectives included:

Exercise Goal:

- Strengthen cybersecurity preparedness and response capabilities by exercising policies, processes, and procedures for identifying and responding to a multi-sector cyber attack targeting critical infrastructure

Exercise Objectives:

- Continue to exercise coordination mechanisms, information sharing efforts, development of shared situational awareness, and decision-making procedures of the cyber incident response community during a cyber event
- Evaluate relevant policy, statutory, and fiscal issues that govern cyber incident response authorities and resource prioritization
- Provide a forum for exercise participants to exercise, evaluate, and improve the processes, procedures, interactions, and information sharing mechanisms within their organization or community of interest
- Assess the role, functions, and capabilities of DHS and other government entities in a cyber event

Exercise Participation

CS V exercise execution included more than 1,200 participants, representing entities from the public and private sectors within the United States and abroad. Participants represented nine Cabinet-level departments, eight full-

---

[2] Exercise Planning Team composed of DHS NCEPP and contractor staff; Team led all aspects of planning, execution, and after action

player states[3], 12 International partners, and nearly 70 private sector companies and coordination bodies. Participation focused on the Information Technology (IT), Communications, Healthcare and Public Health (HPH), and Commercial Facilities (Retail Subsector) critical infrastructure sectors, while also incorporating various levels of play from other critical infrastructure sectors. Within HPH, organizations included healthcare providers, health plan providers, pharmaceuticals, medical device manufacturers, and trade associations. The Retail Subsector included participation from big box retailers, e-commerce companies, specialty stores, food and beverage retailers, and department stores.

CS V also included multiple coordination bodies, such as Information Sharing and Analysis Centers (ISAC), Information Sharing and Analysis Organizations (ISAO), and trade associations – including representative bodies for all primary participating sectors. International participation centered around two international coordination bodies, with a focus on Computer Emergency Response Team (CERT) coordination. The eight full player states primarily consisted of those that participated in a Cyber Storm IV (CS IV) tabletop exercise, however the Multi-State-ISAC (MS-ISAC) also involved other states through monitor and respond play.

DHS and the Exercise Planning Team identified and recruited CS V participants through a variety of means, including leveraging previous CS relationships, reaching out to Government and sector coordination bodies (e.g., Sector Specific Agencies [SSAs] and ISACs), and building upon past participation. In some cases, participants reached directly to NCEPP to express interest in participating. The Exercise Planning Team treated all participants as stakeholders, encouraging involvement in defining objectives, developing and applying the scenario conditions, and supporting exercise evaluation. Annex A contains a list of CS V participants.

Key Achievements

CS V served as a catalyst for learning for the cyber incident response community. Through the exercise planning and execution process, participants:

- Exercised response to a significant cyber incident with support from federal, state, private sector, and international organizations;
- Integrated new stakeholders into a CS national-level capstone exercise, including two new sectors and eight new states – expanding their exposure to cyber response exercises, and providing a foundation for future exercise and improvement efforts;
- Provided an avenue for sector coordination bodies, such as ISACs and ISAOs, to test and refine their coordination mechanisms and demonstrate the value of participation or membership;
- Allowed for private sector organizations to use scenario conditions to collaborate on and develop a range potential solutions and discuss these with their government counterparts;
- Raised awareness of attack vectors that may require non-traditional remediation activities (i.e., not blocking), creating a venue for participating organizations to evaluate response options against potential consequences and emphasizing the need for policies and procedures to remain flexible;
- Provided a venue to examine and identify improvements to internal organizational processes and procedures, including how these may feed into sector or national-level response; and
- Increased cyber preparedness of participants – of respondents to the After Action Questionnaire (AAQ) 96% indicated that participation in CS V will help them become better prepared to deal successfully with a cyber incident.

CS V Scenario and Adversary

Players responded to a cyber-specific scenario that leveraged weaknesses in common protocols and services used on the Internet. The scenario included impacts to routing methodology, the Domain Name System (DNS) used to map hostnames to Internet Protocol (IP) addresses, and Public Key Infrastructure (PKI) used to provide authentication and confidentiality. Scenario conditions affected a wide variety of corporate and government systems, medical devices, and payment systems. During scenario play, the malware included a feature that

---

[3] Others state, local, territorial and tribal entities participated through MS-ISAC alerts

bricked infected systems when players blocked against the malicious IPs. Resolution required a coordinated government and private sector response.

The CS V adversaries incorporated real world threat elements and had the resources, capabilities, and intent to carry out sophisticated and pervasive attacks. Multiple adversaries used the impacts to routing, host name mapping, and authentication to design and deliver attacks against exercise participants. In particular, one primary adversary group developed a sophisticated command and control network and allowed supplementary groups to purchase the access necessary to deliver targeted malware specific to certain sectors. This allowed a diverse set of adversary groups to target CS V players.

CS V Findings

Participant feedback and Exercise Planning Team observations recorded throughout the exercise planning, execution, and after action process revealed four high-level findings that affect the cybersecurity community at large. High-level findings and associated discussion incorporate perspectives of CS V participants representing the Federal Government, State and Local Government, coordination bodies, the private sector, and the International community. In particular, the Exercise Planning Team used the exercise Hotwash, Exercise Spot Reports and After Action Questionnaires (AAQ), CS Community after action teleconferences, and the After Action Meeting (AAM) to build out the findings and supporting evidence. Sub-findings and observations support each high-level finding and provide additional detail.

Finding 1:

A current, national-level plan or framework that has widespread buy-in, adoption, and integration would have formalized and optimized cyber incident response during CS V.

1.1 Players responded to the exercise scenario in accordance with internal organizational policies and procedures, external reporting requirements, and coordination mechanisms (e.g., reporting to ISAOs, ISACs, or law enforcement). However, in general, the community lacked a cohesive framework to guide cyber response activities at a national level, particularly regarding escalation processes, decision-making, and development and distribution of large-scale remediation strategies.

1.2 National-level decision bodies, such as the Unified Coordination Group (UCG) and the Cyber Response Group (CRG) convened during the exercise to discuss impacts. The UCG served as a real-time venue for whole of community coordination and discussion, but did not create a forum for synchronizing activities. In the lead-up to CS V and during exercise execution, multiple UCG members expressed confusion regarding the status and validity of a UCG based on uncertainty of the national-level plans in place. During the exercise, confusion existed regarding the thresholds for UCG and CRG activation, membership, roles, and responsibilities. Confusion also existed among the private sector regarding the membership and functionality of the CRG.

1.3 As the exercise unfolded, controller/evaluators (C/E) noted that communications and reporting lacked clarity on the extent of attack impacts. When players provided reporting, they did not use quantifiable impact assessments to provide a clear understanding of the relative effects across their organizations. This affected understanding of the risks at an industry and ultimately national level, challenging players' ability to assess the severity of the attacks, to manage the risks, and to determine the potential cascading impacts. It also challenged the ability to develop an accurate common operating picture and foster effective decision-making.

1.4 CS V exercised response to a scenario that required non-traditional technical recommendations to limit the impacts of the malware (i.e., outside of "blocking" and "tackling" approaches). Many players executed their normal response activities, blocking against malicious traffic, and worsening the scenario impacts. This highlighted the importance of leveraging risk management principles to inform response strategies.

Finding 1 Observations:

During Cyber Storm III (CS III) in late 2010, stakeholders evaluated the recently completed Interim Version of the National Cyber Incident Response Plan (NCIRP).[4] Participants found that the NCIRP provided a sound framework for steady-state and cyber incident response, but the supporting processes, procedures, roles, and responsibilities required maturity. In the interim, stakeholder organizations matured their cyber capabilities

---

[4] In CS III, players exercised NCIRP, Interim Version, September 2010

significantly, and expanded the volume and quality of coordination efforts. However, during CS V, the stakeholder community did not have a current, signed, national-level cyber framework to evaluate.

When exercise play reached the national level, players did stand up an NCCIC-led UCG to discuss impacts across participants. During the exercise, the UCG served as a real-time mechanism to coordinate across the stakeholder community, facilitated public and private sector communication, and supported awareness. As policy continues to evolve, it is important to ensure that national cyber coordination mechanisms continue to provide a venue for public and private sector collaboration. Exercise participants also recommended that these mechanisms move beyond information sharing and situational awareness and truly provide a forum to consider response options, make decisions, and designate actions. During the exercise, the UCG did not present or discuss private sector recommendations, including potential resolution options provided by the Communications ISAC. The UCG also did not define a way ahead, leaving participants uncertain of next steps or expectations.

While the UCG Charter identifies the group as a forum to spread awareness and synchronize activities, exercise C/Es observed limited discussion on "actions." Along these lines, UCG participants must have the appropriate level of authority to make decisions and designate response actions. Participants also suggested additional guidance on cadence and membership (i.e., integrating affected parties) would be useful. Participants also expressed confusion about who exactly should be on the UCG. For instance, the UCG had a limited number of pre-existing health and retail members, and participants identified the ability to integrate affected parties as an area for improvement.

Participants expressed confusion over the roles and functions of the CRG, and did not have insight into how the group would share outcomes. The private sector anticipated that the CRG would make executive-level decisions regarding mitigation options; however, the CRG never distributed any official communication. Private sector organizations expressed interest in learning more about the CRG, including how decisions may affect the private sector. Operationally, confusion existed regarding escalation and stand-up in response to scenario conditions, and an initial CRG meeting did not include all members.

During the exercise and after action process, stakeholders identified areas of interest concerning national cyber incident response planning and any forthcoming policies. Specifically, stakeholders discussed the need to improve public and private coordination, ensuring this coordination adds value and creating true forums for decision-making. Multiple participants commented on the lack of clarity around escalation processes, including when to escalate externally, where that information went, and how the overall government escalated during a crisis. Participants also emphasized the importance of addressing regulatory issues and the need to protect people and organizations (i.e., indemnification). Multiple stakeholders also emphasized the importance of leveraging previous public-private work on the NCIRP, to include existing mechanisms and supporting processes when developing forthcoming national-level plans.

Risk management is a key component of cyber planning and the development and execution of response strategies. Cyber incident response plans at all levels (i.e., organizational, sector, and national) must take into account and be applicable to a wide variety of risks and potential mitigation actions. The Exercise Planning Team designed the CS V scenario so that traditional "blocking and tackling" actions only made the issues worse. Many organizations followed typical procedures, blocked against malicious IPs, and ended up with a more challenging problem to solve. Any forthcoming national-level plan or framework should use risk management principles to take into consideration a holistic picture of threats, scenarios, and potential attack vectors – including response strategies where non-traditional actions may be the best course.

Also tied to risk management, participants observed that incident response policies and procedures around communication should emphasize the importance of providing impact assessments. Players noted the difficulty of developing a full understanding of the attacks since communications lacked clear impact assessments. For example, an affected organization communicating that malware infected their business systems is far less effective than indicating that malware infected over half of corporate machines, severely limiting the ability to conduct operations, and requiring manual customer support. The lack of impact assessments in reporting challenged player's ability to develop situational awareness and understand the full risk picture – ultimately affecting the ability to make effective decisions that would mitigate or limit the overall risk.

Finding 2:

Challenges around information sharing – thresholds, paths, speed of sharing, and liability issues – still exist and need targeted attention.

2.1 Exercise play highlighted the value of formalized communications paths between public and private, and areas that could benefit from more formalized sharing paths. In particular, sector- and state-focused information sharing and analysis organizations provided an effective conduit. Participants emphasized that for voluntary public and private information sharing to be effective it must have a clear value proposition, where both parties derive value.

2.2 The CS V exercise scenario emphasized potential issues with automated information or indicator sharing. Participants stressed the importance of validating information prior to distribution and or making changes based on that information.

2.3 Scenario play highlighted the need for information and reporting with context and analysis, moving beyond simply providing technical and tactical information. In particular, the government's information sharing process primarily focuses on "Indicators of Compromise" (IOC) and "Indicators of Attack" (IOA) (e.g., IP addresses, hash values, and filenames).

2.4 Over the course of exercise play, players observed that delays in information sharing impacted shared situational awareness. During the exercise, multiple organizations waited for a 100% solution (or 100% understanding of impacts) prior to releasing information. In some cases, sharing a 60% solution or incomplete picture, may still provide value. In these cases, the organization should caveat information as not fully vetted or complete.

2.5 Proactive outreach to law enforcement, intelligence, or other information-sharing partners to report threat indicators or organizational impacts improved the timeliness of subsequent reporting, augmented the report content, and improved the ability to implement a more effective response strategy.

2.6 During the exercise, C/Es noted inconsistencies with alert markings that hindered information sharing. For example, one entity distributed remediation information with markings that allowed for wide distribution and another entity distributed similar information with markings that did not allow for further distribution.

2.7 Many players expressed confusion or lack of understanding on the thresholds for external information sharing, to whom they should share the information externally, and the mechanisms available to share that information.

2.8 Player organizations identified enhancements to their internal information sharing practices. For example, some players reported that their departments actively shared information internally, but did not reach out to other departments, resulting in a lack of awareness across multiple impacted departments and an incomplete understanding of the breadth of the organizational impact. In addition, without sharing information across departments, different groups took separate actions to address the threat and impacts, leading to an asymmetrical and uncoordinated response.

Finding 2 Observations:

Exercise participants agreed upon the inherent value of information sharing and collaboration and identified aspects of sharing to improve based on exercise play. Effective information sharing should inform risk management actions and mitigate against negative effects having regional, national, or global impact. In particular, participants identified uncertain sharing thresholds, limited contextual sharing, delayed information sharing, unclear value propositions, and legal or liability concerns to be the primary challenges during exercise play. Improvements to these areas should focus on better informing risk management decisions and actions.

Participants emphasized that effective, voluntary information sharing first requires a value proposition benefiting both sides. This drives defining information sharing criteria, identifying escalation procedures, and leads to a more integrated response to a global cyber incident. Private sector players expressed concern or hesitated to report issues to the government, specifically around impacts and effects, as the issues continued to manifest and they did not yet fully understand the incident scope. However, during the exercise, several organizations with pre-existing relationships shared information on impacts, helping victims to both understand their peers' perspective and the overall breadth of attacks. In addition, multiple organizations reported into their ISAC or ISAO. From there, the ISACs coordinated with each other and the government, helping members gain insight into attacks occurring elsewhere and allowing the ISACs to pass that information back out through coordination calls or products. These activities and communications provided additional information to consider as players managed the risks to their organizations.

The exercise highlighted the potential dangers of automated sharing or sharing without context – as well as an appetite for situational awareness products or mechanisms that provide analysis. Improved tools and technology support increased automated indicator sharing; however, the CS V scenario highlighted the importance of validation prior to sharing externally or taking action internally. For instance, automated sharing of scenario indicators (e.g., malicious IP addresses) may have worsened scenario impacts if recipients blocked against them immediately. Participants observed a low risk tolerance and a high action bias for Federal network defenders; players defaulted to blocking suspicious or malicious traffic, rather than observing and analyzing the traffic. The scenario highlighted issues with indicator-focused sharing and the need to move beyond indicators in order to provide context. One participant observed that while their organization received a significant amount of tactical information, players still found it difficult to assemble the pieces into a larger picture. Multiple participants echoed this interest in additional focus on analytical sharing.

While there is definitive value in information sharing during a cyber incident, participants recognized that understanding what, when, and with whom to share remains a challenge. During a cyber incident with the scope and scale of the CS V scenario, over-sharing could be detrimental, especially if organizations do not possess the capability to analyze information. Information is valuable if it can be analyzed and result in action, however, over-sharing during an incident may overload responders, creating additional "fog of war" effects.

Law enforcement, intelligence, and information sharing partners praised proactive outreach efforts. Rather than waiting for these partners to disseminate information or official notifications, some players actively reached out to report. These partners reflected positively on the outreach and encouraged organizations to report threat indicators to intelligence sharing partners early on rather than awaiting an official notification. This practice can help organizations more effectively assess and respond to the situation.

Discussions during the planning process and actions taken over the course of execution exposed the realities private sector organizations encounter when sharing incident, threat, and/or mitigation information externally. Though during execution some companies did successfully share incident information, other companies still reserved particular information at the request of their General Counsel or Senior Leadership due to the sensitive nature of the information and its potential impact.

Participants identified information sharing challenges and areas for improvement within their own organizations. For instance, multiple organizations observed that their players struggled with the thresholds for information sharing. This included reaching across internal departments, as well as reaching externally to other organizations. In many cases, organizations can benefit from pre-defined parameters on types of information to share, sharing guidelines, and distribution cadence. Separately, the exercise promoted awareness and created information sharing relationships within organizations. For example, the exercise created awareness of roles and responsibilities, shed light on information needs, and established relationships between information security, legal, public affairs, and management personnel.

Finding 3:

CS V players displayed increased awareness of the NCCIC's role in information sharing and shared situational awareness and increasingly looked to DHS, the NCCIC, and US-CERT to coalesce information and provide reporting back out. DHS and the NCCIC should build upon this and continue to improve their processes, procedures, and overall capabilities.

3.1 Players accepted the NCCIC as the mission coordinator during the incident. The NCCIC was in its nascent stages during CS III and CS IV, but during CS V, the players looked to the NCCIC to distribute alerts and reporting and to coordinate across affected parties. DHS NCCIC should continue to improve internal and external processes for coalescing information, conducting analysis, developing reporting, and distributing it to stakeholders.

3.2 The exercise highlighted the benefits of strong, well-established relationships as well as areas where NCCIC and DHS stakeholder relationships can improve. For example, CS V highlighted strong interagency partnerships and the benefits of having co-located partner liaisons at the NCCIC to share information and reporting. It also highlighted the need to continue strengthening relationships with private sector entities, potentially leveraging coordination bodies (e.g., ISACs), to improve two way sharing.

3.3 As the cyber incident response community expands, specific sectors can benefit from awareness campaigns highlighting how community members report information, when they should report this information (i.e., thresholds), and what types of products and services are available. In addition to improving stakeholder awareness and augmenting their external resources, these awareness efforts will expand the breadth of information used to inform the common operating picture.

Finding 3 Observations:

Exercise C/Es observed increased awareness of the NCCIC's role in information sharing and shared situational awareness as compared to previously conducted exercises. During exercise play, the NCCIC and US-CERT received a high volume of information and reporting. Within the UCG, in particular, participants engaged in robust discussion led by NCCIC personnel. Of the AAQ respondents, 53% reported that the NCCIC provided some level of effectiveness during the simulated response to a cyber incident, indicating that general awareness of the function and capabilities housed within the NCCIC has continued to increase.

However, particularly in the participating sectors, some participants did express uncertainty on the NCCIC's role, what resources it could provide (e.g., products, alerts, or assistance), and how best to interact. Prior to the exercise, many of these organizations had not previously interacted with the NCCIC in the real world. In many cases, CS V did provide awareness to build upon moving forward. The NCCIC should continue to engage with stakeholders, promote capabilities and resources, and spread awareness of critical information sharing requirements so that cyber incident responders understand how the center can help.

Many exercise participants expected to receive products, including analytical products (e.g., advisories with recommendations), during the incident. Although the NCCIC and US-CERT generated Information Bulletins (IB) and Malware Initial Findings Reports (MIFR) for distribution, participants looked to the NCCIC to release alerts more frequently or at a more regular tempo during the incident. As discussed in Finding 2, participants expressed interest moving beyond technical and tactical information products and more towards analytical products with recommendations. NCCIC C/Es observed that NCCIC had a limited capacity to meet these needs during the exercise; however, this could provide an area for future improvement.

The exercise highlighted areas where the NCCIC has strong relationships, in particular across the interagency and through partner liaison officers. For example, having an MS-ISAC representative on the NCCIC floor effectively tied in that organization and, ultimately, all of the member states. During the exercise, and in line with real world responsibilities, DHS and NCCIC players focused efforts on the .gov domain, leading the protection of Federal civilian agencies in cyberspace. Private sector collaboration and information sharing is voluntary. Some private sector players received NCCIC and US-CERT reporting and some players reported information into the NCCIC (largely via third party bodies), but in general, controllers observed these communications to be uneven.

Finding 4:

As first time Cyber Storm exercise participants, the Healthcare and Public Health Sector and the Retail Subsector both observed the value of increased coordination within the sector, expanded information sharing across affected sectors, and the value of more formalized coordination and reporting mechanisms through entities such as ISACs or ISAOs.

4.1 In both sectors, players recognized the value of continuing to use sector coordination bodies and further maturing information sharing and coordination processes. Leveraging formalized information sharing paths simplifies the process and promotes wider distribution and awareness.

4.2 Participants identified the benefits of working across sectors, especially as common attack vectors affect multiple organizations. In addition, HPH and Retail can benefit from coordination with sectors with more established and mature sector coordinating models for cyber incident response.

4.3 Multiple planners and players recognized the value of facilitating relationships across the sector, with coordinating bodies such as ISACs, and with Federal Government reporting. Exercise play highlighted the value of many Federal Government products such as the US-CERT alerts and the Joint Information Bulletins (JIB).

Finding 4 Observations:

The HPH Sector and the Retail Subsector both made significant strides in recent years to mature their cybersecurity stance, including expanding cyber coordination and information sharing activities. During the exercise, some sector organizations coordinated with each other on a one-to-one basis or through sector coordination bodies. Personal relationships or vendor relationships (i.e., pre-incident familiarity) facilitated multiple instances of collaboration and information sharing. However, this coordination did not occur on a sector- or subsector-wide basis.

In some cases, participants identified operational challenges that limited coordination. For example, HPH and Retail both held sector-specific teleconferences during the exercise to share information on the impacts. Not all players affected by the attacks successfully participated, and players experienced some issues with invites and distribution lists. In other cases, C/Es identified challenges related to lack of awareness or limited familiarity with information mechanisms related to a cyber incident. For instance, one participant observed that many players seemed to be "heads-down" trying to isolate the issues and did not perceive the severity of the growing crisis or realize they had external resources (e.g., sector coordination bodies) that may help. However, participants did recognize the value of sector- and subsector-wide coordination and cited participation in CS V as a starting point for future improvement.

Moving forward, participants plan to focus additional efforts on clearing up communications paths and distribution lists. For many participants, CS V constituted their first experience in a large-scale operations-based cyber exercise. In addition to setting the stage for future participation, the exercise play highlighted additional topics to exercise in smaller-scale exercises, including tabletops. For instance, one organization plans to conduct communications exercises to streamline internal processes and promote awareness. Another used the exercise to update their cyber incident response plan, including identifying additional testing topics for the coming years.

CS V also highlighted the benefits of cross-sector coordination. During the exercise, some affected players reached across sectors to share information or request information on attacks or indicators. For example, some organizations reached to their vendors or customers. This outreach helped players to understand the breadth of impacts and informed response actions. In addition, the ISACs coordinated with each other and through the National Council of ISACs to share information and alerts, contributing to improved situational awareness. Outside of incident response coordination, several participants commented that HPH and Retail could benefit from interaction with or mentorship from other more mature sectors, such as Financial or Energy.

HPH, the Retail Subsector, and DHS can do more to collaborate on cyber-specific information sharing and collaboration. As the Sector Specific Agency for the Commercial Facilities Sector, DHS is providing additional cyber-specific support – and emphasizing awareness and education. While HHS is the SSA for HPH, the NCCIC can benefit from closer relationships within the sector and with the NH-ISAC or other coordination bodies. Several HPH entities had limited awareness of DHS cyber resources prior to participating in the exercise. DHS and NCCIC can do more to promote awareness of their capabilities, resources, and information requirements; increasing the value for both the sector and DHS.

Exercise Design Summary

Exercise Planning Construct

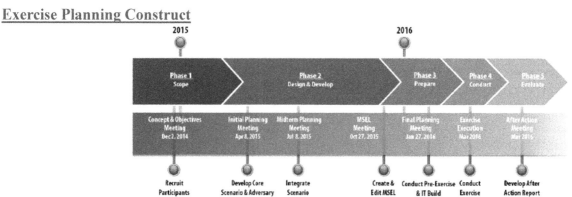

Figure 1: CS V Occurred Over Five Phases

The Exercise Planning Team divided the 18-month planning process into five distinct stages to support the planning, execution, and evaluation of the CS V exercise (Figure 1). Within each stage, a series of events, milestones, and general planning goals moved the process forward. Throughout the process, planners engaged in cross-community interaction, public–private collaboration, and information sharing to support increased awareness and achieve goals for each phase.

Scope Phase

In the initial stages of this phase, DHS and the Exercise Planning Team collaborated on the proposed exercise concept, to include identifying the scope, training objectives, timeline, and potential sectors. Planning efforts focused on establishing the conceptual framework to set the stage for discussions with stakeholders and eventually recruiting. On December 7, 2014, DHS hosted the Concept and Objectives (C&O) Meeting, the first official major planning meeting with stakeholders and participants, to discuss the proposed CS V scope and solicit input. Attendees discussed exercise goals and objectives, planning and execution timeline, participation levels, recruiting targets, scenario options, and exercise structure and design principles. Following this meeting, the Exercise Planning Team initiated recruiting efforts, reengaged previous participants, and continued to define the overall scope based on feedback from the C&O Meeting.

Critical infrastructure sector selection comprised an important milestone in the scope phase. Traditionally, CS exercises include representation from at least two critical infrastructure sectors in addition to traditional IT and Communications sector participants. This participation model brings in new players, strengthens relationships, and improves cyber response plans and capabilities. The sector criteria for CS V included perceived readiness, interest and ability to commit, DHS relationships, IT and Communications dependencies, and a threat analysis of recent attacks and future threats. For instance, the HPH Sector expressed interest in participation dating back to CS I and had consistently ramped up sector coordination activities for cyber planning and response. For the Retail Subsector, a combination of DHS serving as the SSA, standup and advancement in information sharing organizations, and several high profile attacks made it an ideal candidate.

In terms of exercise design and construct, the Exercise Planning Team retained the "CS Community" approach to exercise planning. As participants on boarded, the Exercise Planning Team assigned participants to a more manageable and focused CS Community, each with a dedicated Exercise Planning Team Lead. The CS Communities created forums to discuss common issues, develop objectives, and identify scenario impacts that would challenge their players. The CS V Communities included HPH, Retail, Federal, International, IT/Communications (IT/Comms), Law Enforcement/Intelligence/Department of Defense (LE/I/DoD), PA, and States.

Design and Develop Phase

The Design and Develop Phase comprised the vast majority of the planning process and included three of the five major planning meetings. During this phase, the Exercise Planning Team and organizational planners finalized goals and objectives, defined CS Community objectives and desired conditions, designed the scenario and adversary, and applied these to organizational conditions in order to create scenario injects. In addition, the organizational planners participated in monthly CS Community calls, received virtual training on CS V, and led all organizationally specific aspects of organizational planning.

DHS hosted the Initial Planning Meeting (IPM) on April 8, 2015. Nearly 100 stakeholders from the government and private sector participated in the full-day meeting. The IPM consisted of a series of both plenary and breakout sessions designed to provide information on exercise construct and solicit input on design specifics. For many of the stakeholders, the IPM was the first chance to gain an understanding of the exercise scope and construct. The plenary sessions informed stakeholders of the planning and execution timeline, required milestones, and the levels of participation for the exercise. CS Communities established initial community objectives, plans and policies to examine, and boundaries for their scenarios during the breakout sessions.

Following the IPM, CS V stakeholders identified organization-specific objectives, scenarios of interest, and additional partners and players to recruit for the exercise. The Exercise Planning Team then provided informational briefings to leaders to gain their buy in and commitment to participation. A Scenario Team, comprised of key technical and exercise professionals, began to design the exercise core scenario to serve as the technical basis for exercise play. The Federal Community also stood up immediately following the IPM and consisted of Federal Departments and Agencies as well as the US-CERT and NCCIC. Communities held monthly teleconferences throughout the planning process to provide updates and advance community and scenario development. In many cases, CS Community Leads also held one on one calls with organizations in between monthly calls to conduct more focused working sessions on each organization's exercise play.

On July 8, 2015, DHS hosted the CS V Midterm Planning Meeting (MPM). The MPM, again, included a series of plenary and breakout sessions. Plenary sessions provided information on planning progress and milestones, described the core scenario baseline, initiated community scenario planning, and solicited input on exercise design specifics. The core scenario baseline would become the unifying backstory of the local impacts on each CS Community. The plenary session also included a discussion of what the exercise adversary should look like and how its capabilities might affect the CS Communities, especially LE/I/DoD. At the conclusion of the MPM, DHS provided public affairs guidance for external messaging about CS V to stakeholders.

Stakeholder organizations used the time after the MPM to build out their internal scenarios using the core scenario as a baseline. CS Community Leads assisted organizations with tying the core scenario baseline to common organizational desired conditions via pre-identified scenario linkages. Developing these scenario linkages ensured that the scenarios made logical technical sense and triggered the national level discussions desired by the Exercise Planning Team. They also ensured CS Community members experienced similar conditions to similar systems. Coming out of this process, each organization had a scenario framework established that could be shared with other stakeholders in their community and be further refined into the observable injects presented to players during the exercise.

DHS hosted the CS V Master Scenario Events List (MSEL) Meeting, the fourth of five major planning meetings on October 27, 2015. At the meeting, the Exercise Planning Team led the attendees through both plenary discussions and CS Community-focused breakout sessions. The plenary discussions focused on scenario development, timing, and inject development. The CS Community breakout sessions focused on how the timing of scenario events would fit into the three days of the exercise. During subsequent plenary sessions, all exercise stakeholders discussed the timing of scenarios and cross-community exercise play. Additional MSEL Meeting plenary topics provided planners with information on exercise evaluation and public affairs.

Building on the MSEL Meeting, CS Communities finalized organization-specific scenario narratives. Using the scenario narratives, organization planners identified their player observables and developed time-sequenced exercise injects. The sum of the exercise injects for each organization became the MSEL. In order to be fully prepared for exercise play, planners also identified expected player actions, organizational media play, and simulation requirements for ExCon. CS Community Leads continued to host monthly planning calls as well as individual calls with organizations to update their MSELs in preparation for the Final Planning Meeting (FPM).

Prepare Phase

As the fifth and final major planning meeting, DHS hosted the CS V Final Planning Meeting (FPM) on January 27, 2016. Participants spent the vast majority of the FPM reviewing the CS V exercise MSEL in plenary session. The Exercise Planning Team asked attendees to focus on inject content, timing, cross-community dependencies, and overall compliance with the ground truth. This session ensured that the exercise scenario remained in sync across all communities. As the final major planning meeting, additional FPM briefings focused on exercise logistics and mechanics to prepare planners for exercise execution.

In the final planning phase, CS Community Leads coordinated working sessions with members of the Scenario Team and organizational planners to make edits to and ultimately finalize exercise injects. The Exercise Planning Team supported exercise preparation by providing information on ExCon logistics, assisting with artifact development and 2500 inject review, identifying white cell support roles, finalizing the player directory. The Exercise Planning Team also provided four virtual C/E training sessions and eight sessions of virtual player training. Planner/C/E training sessions provided C/Es with guidelines for observing exercise play and described their roles and responsibilities before, during, and after the exercise. Player training sessions introduced and familiarized players with the exercise and described their role and available resources during the exercise.

Conduct Phase

CS V exercise execution included more than 1,200 participants, representing entities from the public and private sectors within the United States, as well as internationally. Exercise participants included players, C/Es, and ExCon representatives. DHS hosted approximately 90 representatives at CS V ExCon, in Washington, D.C., from March 7 to 11, 2016. ExCon functions included exercise management; flow control; inject review, development, and release; and simulation support. ExCon representatives included full player participants from the public sector, private industry, critical infrastructure sectors, states, and international partners. These representatives helped to manage play at their own organizations through interaction with other ExCon members and contact with their offsite C/Es.

On the first day, ExCon and participants out in the field conducted systems checks, reviewed read-ahead material, and prepared for live exercise play. Live exercise play ran from 0900 on Tuesday, March 8, until 1700 EST on Thursday, March 10. During this time, ExCon distributed more than 1,000 pre-scripted injects via email and phone calls. Players received additional ad hoc injects based on player response and exercise play. The Exercise Website provided a single location for registered users to access NCENN sites, all exercise documentation, the Player Directory, simulated social media, and simulated adversary sites and blogs. The Exercise Planning Team updated all of the simulated sites in real time during the exercise based on dynamic play.

During exercise play, ExCon also facilitated twice-daily "all-ExCon" and C/E teleconferences to summarize scenario play, preview upcoming activity, discuss initial observations, and answer questions. On Friday, March 11, 2016, ExCon representatives, distributed C/Es, and local stakeholders conducted the Hotwash. During the Hotwash, the Exercise Planning Team reviewed overall exercise play and CS Community scenario results, and all participants discussed exercise outcomes and initial findings. The Exercise Planning Team provided additional information on next steps, the after action process, and reminded all participants to submit an AAQ.

Evaluate Phase

The Exercise Planning Team implemented various mechanisms to capture player action, observations, and evaluation input. Participating organizations provided a C/E to monitor and control exercise play from that organization's home location. During the exercise, C/Es reported on scenario development, monitored player interaction, and communicated any issues. They also participated in twice-daily "all-ExCon" and C/E teleconferences to ensure they remained in sync with ExCon and abreast of upcoming scenario activity. The Exercise Planning Team also encouraged C/Es, players,

After Action Questionnaire Highlights

- ✓ 96% of respondents indicated that participation in CS V will help them become better prepared to deal successfully with a cyber incident
- ✓ 85% have cyber incident response plans
- ✓ 84% rated the overall effectiveness of the Federal Government in coordinating a response to the simulated cyber event moderately to highly effective

and ExCon staff to use "Spot Reports," available on the Exercise Website, to capture and submit any quick in-exercise feedback. After live exercise play concluded, DHS encouraged all participants to complete and submit an AAQ. This questionnaire captured responses around key focus areas such as: lessons learned and areas for improvement; information sharing and coordination; implementation of cyber incident response policies, plans, and procedures; roles and capabilities of government entities; and exercise design and execution feedback. The Exercise Planning Team also provided a separate questionnaire for stakeholders to use to update their National Institute of Standards and Technology (NIST) profile.

DHS hosted several after action events to discuss and vet potential findings and to solicit feedback from the participant community. First, each CS Community hosted a teleconference to discuss community-specific findings, capture specific observations, and identify how the community interacted within the exercise community at large. On April 5, 2016, DHS hosted the AAM for all exercise participants both in-person at DHS and via teleconference. During the meeting, attendees reviewed and provided input to high-level findings, sub-findings, and recommendations for improvement. Following the AAM, the Exercise Planning Team provided participants with several opportunities for review and edit to the after action documentation.

Conclusion

CS V provided a realistic environment for our national cyber response apparatus to assess cyber incident response capabilities. DHS and participating organizations worked closely to establish the exercise's goal and objectives and design a realistic scenario that allowed stakeholders to address both organizational and national-level objectives. The resulting scenario allowed the community to coordinate a national-level response to a significant cyber incident. As part of exercise play, players identified significant findings and actions at the national, state, sector, and organizational level that the cyber response community should address. Ultimately, CS V served as a tool that allowed the stakeholder community to examine the evolution of cyber response capabilities and identify current gaps and challenges in responding to a coordinated cyber attack with global impacts. As a result, stakeholders have the opportunity to address these findings and bolster cyber response capabilities at an organizational-level, increasing the preparedness of the nation as a whole.

ANNEX A. PARTICIPANT LIST

Cyber Storm V Participants

Federal Government Entities

- Department of Commerce (Commerce)
- Department of Defense (DoD)
  - Chief Information Officer (CIO)
  - Defense Cyber Crime Center (DC3)
  - Defense Health Agency (DHA)
  - Intelligence Community Security Coordination Center (IC-SCC)
  - National Security Agency (NSA) Threat Operations Center (NTOC)
  - North American Aerospace Defense Command (NORAD)-United States Northern Command (USNORTHCOM)
  - United States Cyber Command (USCYBERCOM)
- Department of Health and Human Services (HHS)
  - Food and Drug Administration (FDA)
    - Office of Criminal Investigations (OCI)
  - Office of Security and Strategic Information (OSSI)
  - Office of the Assistant Secretary for Preparedness and Response (ASPR)
  - Office of the Chief Information Officer (OCIO)
    - Computer Security Incident Response Center (CSIRC)
  - Office of the National Coordinator for Health Information Technology (ONC)
- Department of Homeland Security (DHS)
  - Federal Emergency Management Agency (FEMA)
  - National Protection and Programs Directorate (NPPD)
    - Office of Infrastructure Protection (IP)
      - Commercial Facilities Sector Specific Agency (SSA)
      - National Infrastructure Coordinating Center (NICC)
    - Office of Cybersecurity and Communications (CS&C)
      - National Cybersecurity and Communications Integration Center (NCCIC)
        - Industrial Control Systems Cyber Emergency Response Team (ICS-CERT)
        - National Coordinating Center for Communications (NCC)
        - NCCIC Liaison Officers (LNO)
        - United States Computer Emergency Readiness Team (US-CERT)
      - Office of External Affairs
      - Office of International Affairs (OIA)
      - Stakeholder Engagement and Cyber Infrastructure Resilience (SECIR)
  - Office of Intelligence and Analysis (I&A)
  - Office of Public Affairs (OPA)
  - United States Customs and Border Protection (CBP)
  - United States Secret Service (USSS)
- Department of Justice (DOJ)
  - Federal Bureau of Investigation (FBI)
- Department of Transportation (DOT)
  - Federal Aviation Administration (FAA)
    - Security Operations Center (SOC)
- Department of Treasury (Treasury)
- Department of Veterans Affairs (VA)
- Federal Communications Commission (FCC)
- White House/National Security Council (NSC) Staff

State Government Entities

- Alabama
  - Huntsville Utilities
- Arkansas
  - Saline County

- California
  - Alameda Municipal Power
  - California State Threat Assessment Center
  - City of Healdsburg
  - City of Hemet
  - Sacramento County
  - Sacramento Municipal Utility District
  - San Diego Law Enforcement Coordination Center
  - San Luis Obispo County
- Colorado
  - Jefferson County
- Florida
  - Agency for Health Care Administration
  - Agency for Persons with Disabilities
  - Agency for State Technology
  - City of Tampa
  - Collier County
  - Division of Administrative Hearings
  - Executive Office of the Governor
  - Florida Attorney General's Office
  - Florida Commission on Human Relations
  - Florida Commission on Offender Review
  - Florida Department of Agriculture and Consumer Services
  - Florida Department of Business and Professional Regulation
  - Florida Department of Children and Families
  - Florida Department of Citrus
  - Florida Department of Corrections
  - Florida Department of Economic Opportunity
  - Florida Department of Education
  - Florida Department of Elder Affairs
  - Florida Department of Environmental Protection
  - Florida Department of Financial Services
  - Florida Department of Health
  - Florida Department of Juvenile Justice
  - Florida Department of Law Enforcement
  - Florida Department of Management Services
  - Florida Department of Revenue
  - Florida Department of State
  - Florida Department of Transportation
  - Florida Department of Veterans' Affairs
  - Florida Division of Emergency Management
  - Florida Fish and Wildlife Conservation Commission
  - Florida Highway Safety and Motor Vehicles
  - Florida Office of Early Learning
  - Florida State Lottery
  - Palm Beach County
  - Public Service Commission
- Georgia
  - City of Rome
  - Georgia Bureau of Investigation
  - Georgia Department of Administrative Services
  - Georgia Department of Behavioral Health and Developmental Disabilities
  - Georgia Department of Community Health
  - Georgia Department of Corrections
  - Georgia Department of Defense
  - Georgia Department of Driver Services

- o Georgia Department of Human Services
- o Georgia Department of Juvenile Justice
- o Georgia Department of Natural Resources
- o Georgia Department of Public Health
- o Georgia Department of Revenue
- o Georgia Emergency Management Agency
- o Georgia Information Sharing Analysis Center
- o Georgia Secretary of State
- o Georgia Technology Authority
  - Georgia Enterprise Technology Services
  - Portal Group
- o Governor's Office of Planning and Budget
- o Harbin Clinic
- o State Accounting Office
- Idaho
  - o Idaho Office of the Chief Information Officer
  - o Latah County
- Louisiana
- Illinois
  - o Village of Westmont
- Maine
  - o Maine Department of Education
  - o Maine Department of Health and Human Services – Data, Research, and Vital Statistics
  - o Maine Emergency Management Agency
  - o Maine Office of Information Technology
- Maryland
  - o Calvert County
- Mississippi
  - o Mississippi Department of Human Services
  - o Mississippi Department of Information Technology Services
  - o Mississippi Department of Medicaid
  - o Mississippi Department of Transportation
  - o Mississippi State Department of Health
- Missouri
  - o City of Springfield
  - o Missouri Department of Social Services
  - o Missouri Office of Administration
  - o Missouri State Highway Patrol
- Montana
  - o Missoula County
- Nebraska
  - o Omaha Public Power District
- Nevada
  - o Nevada Department of Administration
    - Enterprise IT Services Division
  - o Nevada Department of Health and Human Services
    - Division of Public and Behavioral Health
    - Division of Welfare and Supportive Services
  - o Nevada Department of Public Safety
    - Division of Emergency Management
    - General Services Division
    - Nevada Threat Analysis Center
  - o Nevada Department of Taxation
- New Hampshire
  - o City of Nashua
- New Jersey

- o Township of Hillsborough
- New York
  - o New York State Office of Information Technology Services
  - o Sea Gate Police Department
- North Dakota
- Ohio
  - o Wood County
- Oklahoma
  - o Office of the Governor
  - o Oklahoma Office of Management and Enterprise Services
  - o Oklahoma State Regents for Higher Education-OneNet
- Oregon
  - o Oregon Department of Administrative Services
    - ▪ Oregon Office of the State Chief Information Officer – Enterprise Security Office
    - ▪ Oregon Office of the State Chief Information Officer – Enterprise Technology Services
    - ▪ Public Information Office
  - o Oregon Health Authority/Department of Human Services
  - o Oregon Office of Emergency Management
  - o Oregon Office of the Governor
  - o Oregon Parks and Recreation Department
  - o Port of Portland
- Pennsylvania
  - o Penn State Milton S. Hershey Medical Center
- South Carolina
- South Dakota
  - o City of Brookings
- Texas
  - o Department of Information Resources
- Washington
  - o City of Bellevue
  - o City of Blaine
  - o Port of Seattle
- Washington, D.C.
  - o Washington Regional Threat Analysis Center
- West Virginia
- Wisconsin
  - o City of Fond du Lac
  - o Forest County
  - o Village of Pleasant Prairie
- Wyoming
  - o Division of Criminal Investigation
  - o Office of Homeland Security
  - o Wyoming Department of Enterprise Technology
  - o Wyoming Department of Health

Industry Entities

- Aetna
- Amazon
- Amgen
- Army and Air Force Exchange Service (AAFES)
- AT&T
- Bayer HealthCare
- BevMo!
- Books-A-Million
- CenturyLink

Cyber Storm V Participants

- Cox
- CVS Health
- Demandware
- Dominos
- DSW
- GE Healthcare
- HealthPlan Services
- Intermountain Healthcare
- J. Crew
- Juniper Networks
- Liquor Control Board of Ontario (LCBO)
- McKesson
- Macy's
- Mandiant/FireEye
- Major Banking and Finance Company
- Medtronic
- Merck & Co
- Mount Sinai Health System
- Palo Alto Networks
- PayPal
- PFSWeb
- Philips Healthcare
- Recreational Equipment, Inc.(REI)
- Siemens Healthcare
- Sprint
- St. Luke's Health System
- Stanford Health Care
- Surescripts
- Tallahassee Memorial HealthCare
- Target
- Time Warner Cable
- Toshiba America Medical Systems
- Ulta
- Verizon
- Virtua
- Walmart

Coordination Bodies

- Advanced Medical Technology Association
- America's Health Insurance Plans (AHIP)
- American Hospital Association (AHA)
- College of Healthcare Information Management Executives (CHIME)
- Communications Information Sharing and Analysis Center (Comms-ISAC)
- Cyber Response Group (CRG)
- ECRI Institute
- Financial Services Information Sharing and Analysis Center (FS-ISAC)
- Health Information Trust Alliance (HITRUST)
- Healthcare Information and Management Systems Society (HIMSS)
- Healthcare and Public Health Sector Coordinating Council
- Information Technology Information Sharing and Analysis Center (IT-ISAC)
- Medical Device Innovation, Safety and Security Consortium (MDISS)
- Medical Device Manufacturers Association (MDMA)
- Medical Imaging & Technology Alliance (MITA)

Cyber Storm V Participants
• Multi-State Information Sharing and Analysis Center (MS-ISAC) • National Health Information Sharing and Analysis Center (NH-ISAC) • National Retail Federation (NRF) • Retail Cyber Intelligence Sharing Center (R-CISC)   o Retail & Commercial Services Information Sharing and Analysis Center • Retail Industry Leaders Associate (RILA) • The Joint Commission • Unified Coordination Group (UCG)

International Entities

- Australia
  - o CERT-Australia
- Canada
  - o Public Safety Canada (PS Canada)
- Denmark
  - o Centre for Cyber Security (CFCS)
- Finland
  - o National Cyber Security Centre Finland (NCSC-FI)
- Germany
  - o CERT-Bund (BSI)
- Hungary
  - o GovCERT-Hungary
- Japan
  - o Japan Computer Emergency Response Team Coordination Center (JPCERT/CC)
  - o National Information Security Center (NISC)
- Netherlands
  - o National Cyber Security Centrum (NCSC)
- New Zealand
  - o National Cyber Security Centre (NCSC)
- Sweden
  - o Swedish Civil Contingencies Agency (MSB)
- Switzerland
  - o Reporting and Analysis Centre for Information Assurance (MELANI/GovCERT.ch)
- United Kingdom
  - o CERT-UK